VALERIE CAPERS

PORTRAITS IN JAZZ

A PIANO ALBUM

MUSIC DEPARTMENT

OXFORD
UNIVERSITY PRESS

PORTRAITS IN JAZZ

CONTENTS

Portraits in Jazz

For Piano

Valerie Capers

1. Ella Scats the Little Lamb

Bright and spirited (all accents to be carefully observed)

Printed by Halstan Printing Group, Amersham.

4

2. Waltz for Miles

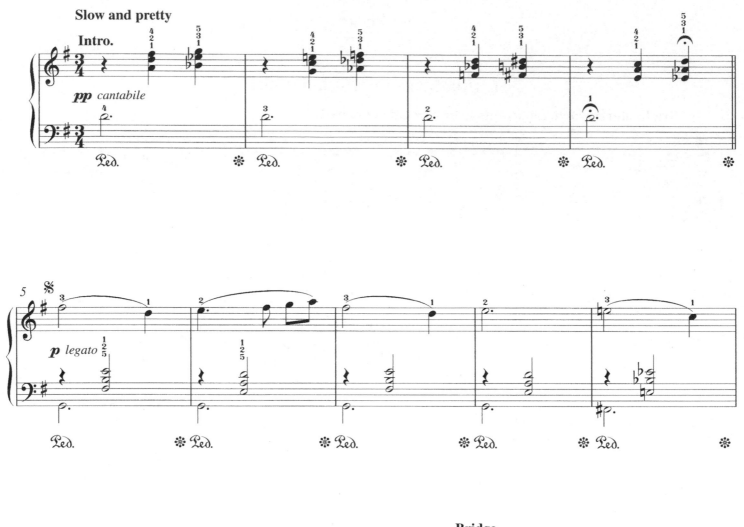

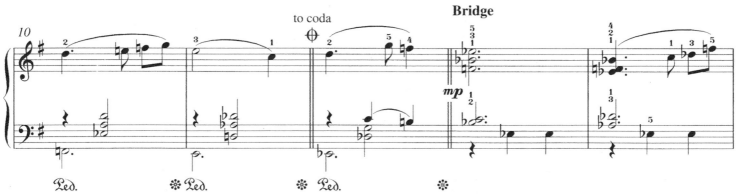

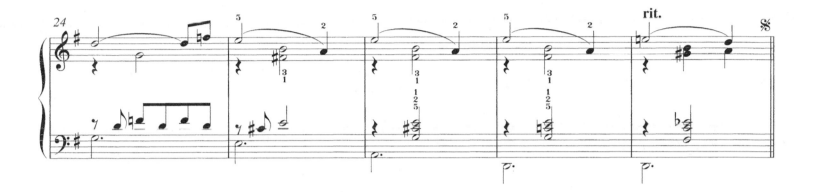

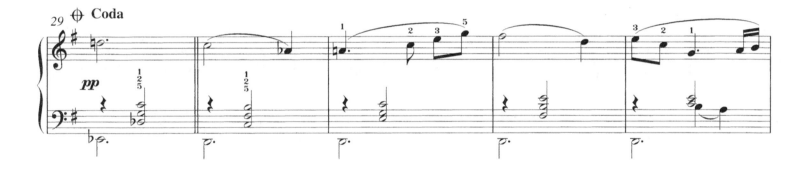

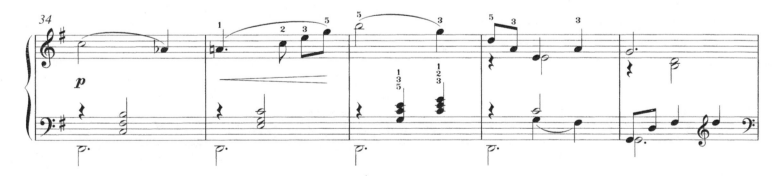

3. Sweet Mister Jelly Roll

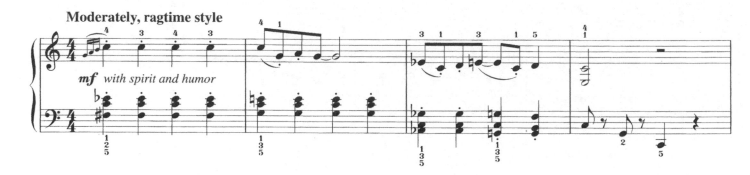

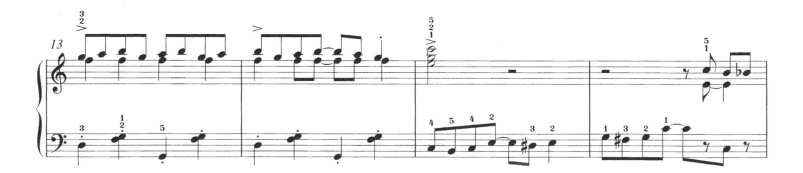

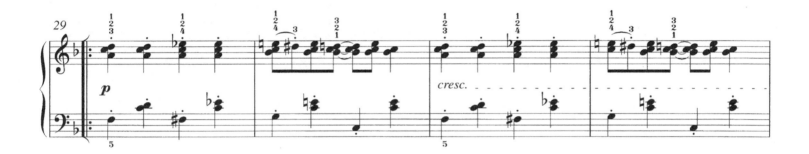

8

4. The Monk

Moderato, in a playful and joking manner

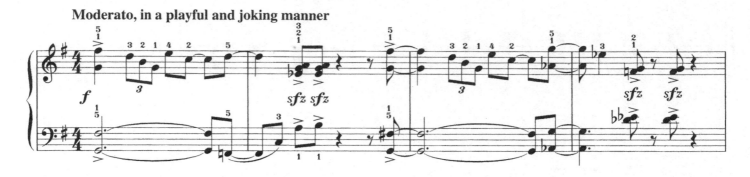

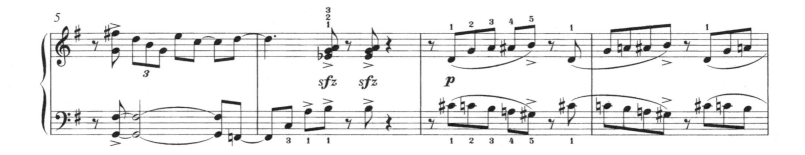

5. Blues for "The Duke"

Laid back, lazy, and somewhat mournful
1st Chorus

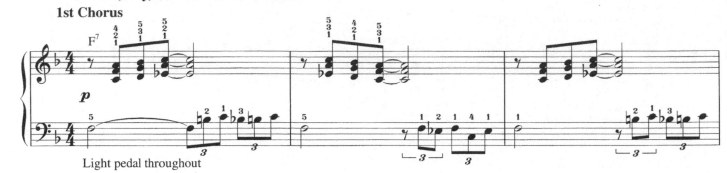

Light pedal throughout

to coda

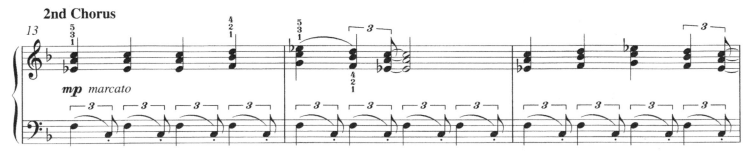

2nd Chorus

3rd Chorus

D.C. al ⊕ ⊕ **Coda**

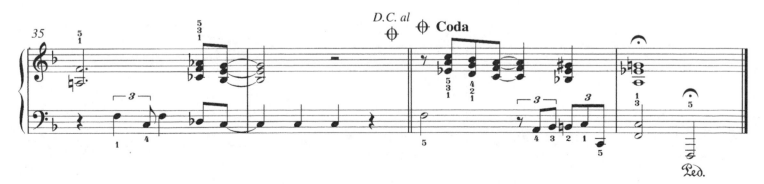

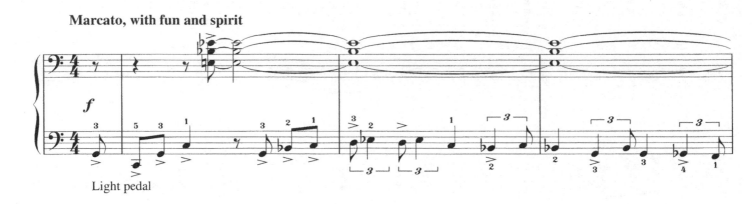

6. A Taste of Bass

Marcato, with fun and spirit

f

Light pedal

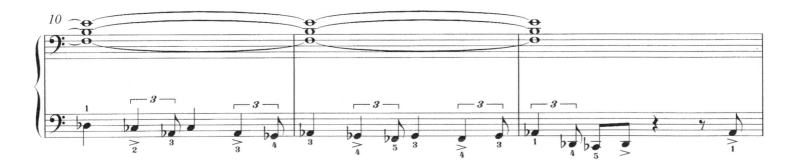

7. Billie's Song

Andante cantabile con moto

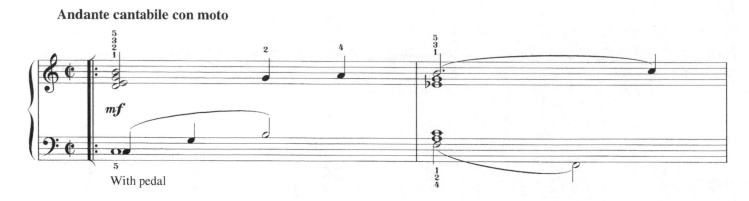

With pedal

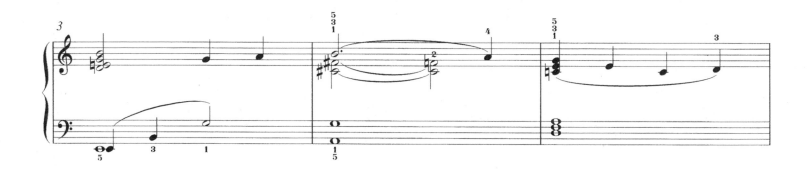

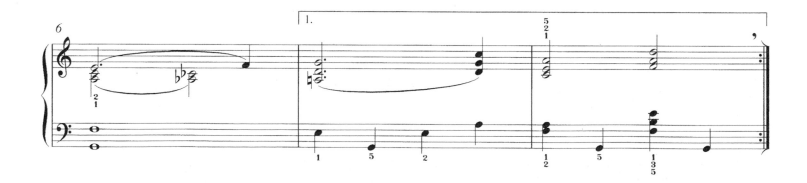

Bridge

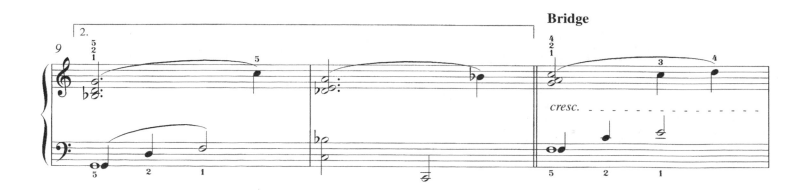

cresc.

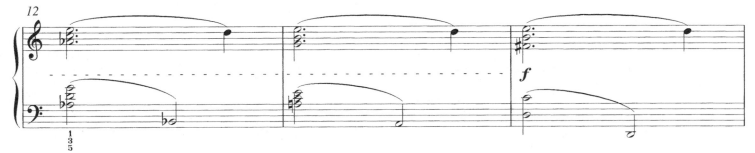

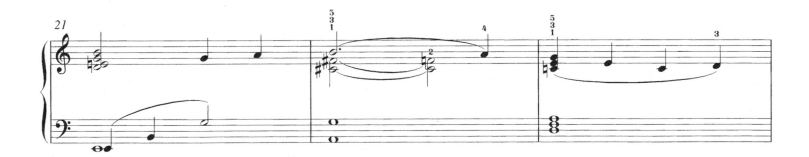

8. Mr. "Satchmo"

Moderate tempo, with a relaxed swing

L.H. legato unless otherwise indicated

rit.　　　　　　a tempo

8vb

9. Canción de la Havana

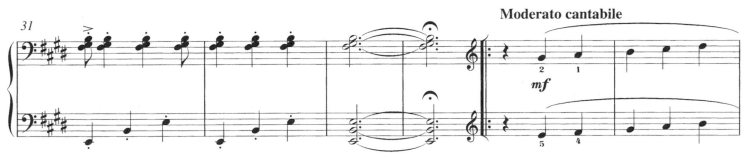

Moderato cantabile

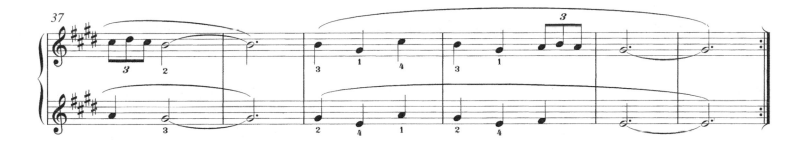

Allegro vivace

una corda

10. Bossa Brasilia

Intro
Easy tempo (moderato cantabile)

mp

Light pedal throughout

mp

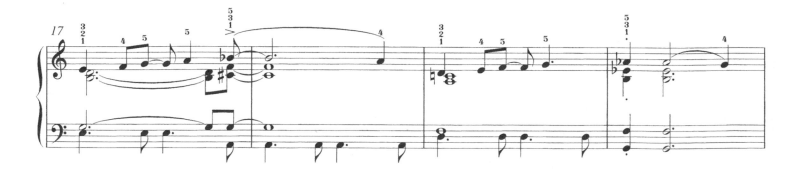

11. Blue-Bird

Fast and bright ($\mathbf{\circ}$ = 76)

1st Chorus

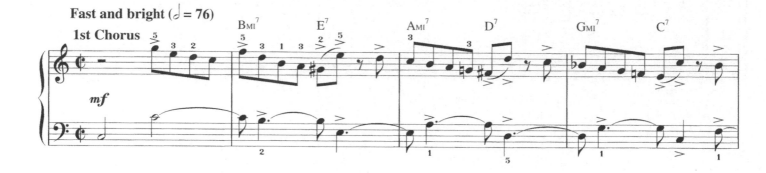

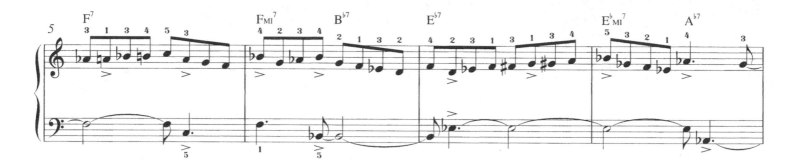

2nd Chorus

3rd Chorus

Coda

12. Cool-Trane

Briskly and with vigor ($\downarrow$ = 120)

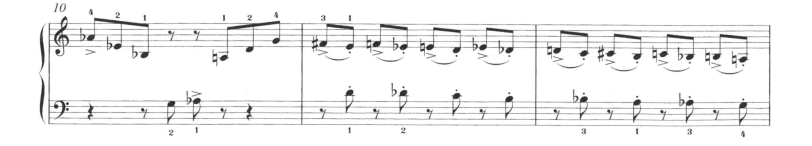

Light pedal to the end

A GUIDE TO INTERPRETATION

Ella Scats the Little Lamb

Ella Fitzgerald is considered by many to be the greatest scat singer of all time. Scat singing is a style of improvising a melodic line using made-up syllables or sounds that often imitate the style of instrumental performers.

Think of this piece as a little two-part invention. The left hand should be quiet and basically legato against the right hand, which plays a melodic variation of the tune *Mary Had a Little Lamb*.

Waltz for Miles

Miles Davis was unique in his treatment of a beautiful melody. His creativity and extraordinary sensitivity to phrase and his beautiful soft trumpet sound made his playing of a ballad unforgettable.

In *Waltz for Miles* a simple melody floats over warm, impressionistic harmonies—just the sort of song that might catch Mr. Davis's fancy. Make the melody in the right hand prominent and lyrical, and be sure to give the whole piece careful light pedaling.

Sweet Mister Jelly Roll

This piece makes no attempt to imitate the piano style of the great Jelly Roll Morton, but rather tries to recreate in the simplest way the sound and style of ragtime piano. Throughout the piece the left hand plays a simplified version of stride bass, one of the defining techniques of ragtime and swing piano.

Play with great spirit and humor, but always remember the words of Scott Joplin: "It is never right to play ragtime fast."

The Monk

Thelonious Monk's piano style was unmistakably individual. To hear him play just once was to know his sound forever more.

In playing this piece, bring out the open fifths and sevenths, the biting seconds, the off-balance accents and the tightly clustered chords—all important parts of the Monk sound—and pay strict attention to all accents and phrase marks. In bars 7–9 there is a quote from Monk's famous blues called *Straight No Chaser*.

Blues for "The Duke"

This piece is written in the traditional twelve-bar blues form, and the melody and harmonies in bars 1–12 are reminiscent of some of Duke Ellington's early compositions. Traditional blues is based on three chords—the I, IV, and V chords of a key (here, F, B-flat, and C; they are marked for you in the opening section).

Think of this blues as a theme (bars 1–12) with two sets of twelve-bar variations, with a return to the opening theme, like the classical *aria da capo*. Play the left hand softly and quietly. The melody is in the top notes of the right-hand chords; it is important to bring them out clearly.

A Taste of Bass

A Taste of Bass features the left hand. Like a bass player—far too often the unsung hero of a jazz combo—the pianist's left hand rarely gets to shine melodically, since it usually provides the rhythmic and harmonic foundation for the composition. Here the left hand plays what we call a "line" rather than a traditional melody. The first seventeen bars comprise a miniature bass solo. In bars 18–24, the left hand has a special kind of line called a *walking bass line* (play it and you'll see why).

To capture the swing and spirit of this piece, you should observe all the accents very carefully, and work to make your left-hand playing just as crisp and snappy as your right. The function of the bass is to create energy and movement. Ron Carter's solos and rhythm work had a profound effect on his generation of bass players and his sense of time, tone, and technique was described as brilliant.

Billie's Song

This is a pretty ballad dedicated in fondest memory to the great lady of song, Billie Holiday. "Lady Day," as she was called, had a special warmth and intensity about her. Her singing was an unforgettable experience due to so much sadness and tragedy in her personal life.

The lyrical melody should stand out above the accompanying harmonies. Pedal carefully, keeping a singing legato while making the chord changes clean and clear.

Mr. "Satchmo"

This piece attempts to capture the feeling of the old New Orleans street bands, whose charm and simplicity are typical of early American jazz and hallmarks of the tradition from which Louis Armstrong came.

Don't play the piece too fast! New Orleans is called The Big Easy, and a traditional New Orleans band struts and dances more than it marches. Besides, you'll need the time for the fast triplets in bars 15–16 and 23–24, which imitate a Louis Armstrong cadential break. In bars 3–4, 7–8, and other similar phrases that follow, the right hand line imitates the style of Satchmo's early trumpet-playing.

Canción de la Havana

Dedicated to the great Afro-Cuban percussionist Mongo Santamaria, *Canción de la Havana* is based primarily on a Nigerian rhythm, one of many West-African rhythmic patterns basic to the Afro-Cuban idiom, but the piece also has a strong feeling of spontaneity and improvisation reminiscent of Spanish flamencan music, especially in bars 1–7 and 23–25, where the broken chords imitate the style of the flamencan guitar. The style of guaguanco music, a combination of West-African and flamencan influences, can be heard in bars 38–53.

Play the first thirteen measures freely, as if you were improvising. To avoid difficulty in coordinating the rhythms between the right and left hand in bars 14–21, practice this passage separately as a keyboard exercise, or on a table-top as a two-hand rhythmic drill.

Bossa Brasilia

The bossa nova (new beat), a two-measure rhythmic pattern in cut time from Brazil, greatly influenced American pop music and jazz during the 1960s and continues to be an important part of those musical idioms. *Bossa Brasilia* suggests the flavor and feeling of the bossa nova through the repetition of the dotted-quarter-and-eighth-note pattern in the left hand, played against the offbeat quarter-notes of the melody in the right hand.

In playing bossa nova, always make the melody smooth and lyrical, and keep the left hand quiet underneath it. Think of spinning out the melody in four-bar phrases against half-bar rhythmic pulse in the left hand.

Blue-Bird

A modern or chromatic blues consisting of twelve bars—like the traditional blues, but greatly expanded harmonically, with one or two chord changes in every bar—*Blue-Bird* is in bebop style with an extended melodic line, coupled together with subtle rhythmic complexities. At first, you may feel the music is rhythmically lopsided, but don't be afraid to stress the off-beat lines and chords in the left hand. These create the feeling of swing and movement that define bebop.

Think of *Blue-Bird* as a miniature theme and variations, with the first chorus as the theme and choruses 2 and 3 as variations, rounded off with a return to the theme and a short coda.

Carefully observe all accents, but make sure to keep the lines legato, so the phrases hold together clearly.

I dedicate this piece to Charlie "Bird" Parker, whose saxophone playing created a whole new world in jazz.

Cool-Trane

The title, of course, is a play on the name of the great saxophone player John Coltrane. To jazz musicians, "cool" is just about the highest compliment you can pay to a fellow musician's talent and ability, and Coltrane was one of the coolest of the cool. There is a quote from Coltrane's blues *Cousin Mary* in bars 17–20.

Because of its saxophone-like melodic line passing from hand to hand, close hand-positions, and sparse texture, *Cool-Trane* is the biggest technical challenge in this collection. For the most part it is made up of two-bar phrases that may feel awkward and hard to connect at first, but will quickly fall into place if you pay close attention to the accents and to the repetitions of a few basic patterns. In order to facilitate control, you should memorize not only the notes, but also the physical feel of each new two-bar phrase. Use a non-legato touch, but not staccato. In bars 1–10, keep the line continuous, with no break in sound when the melody moves from hand to hand.

ABOUT THE COMPOSER

Dr. Valerie Capers was born in New York City and received her early schooling at the New York Institute for the Education of the Blind. She went on to obtain both her Bachelor's and Master's degrees from the Juilliard School of Music, and was awarded the honorary degree of Doctor of Fine Arts from Susquehanna University. She served on the faculty of the Manhattan School of Music and was chairman of the Department of Music and Art at Bronx Community College of the City University of New York, where she is professor emeritus.

Among the first recipients of Essence Magazine's Women of Essence award, in company with Oprah Winfrey and Marla Gibbs, Capers was the first to win the award for music. She received the prestigious Heritage Award, acknowledging a performer who has contributed an enduring legacy to the American jazz tradition. She has received awards and commissions from the National Endowment for the Arts, Meet the Composer, and the CUNY Research Foundation, and was given a special projects grant presenting famous performers at the Bronx Museum for the Arts.

Influenced by her father's ties to Fats Waller and by her brother, the late Bobby Capers, who played tenor and flute, Capers is equally at home in jazz and in classics. Her jazz compositions include *Sing About Love*, the critically-acclaimed Christmas cantata produced by George Wein at Carnegie Hall, and *Sojourner*, a composition based on the life of Sojourner Truth, performed and staged by the Opera Ebony company of New York. Her *Song of the Seasons*, for voice, cello, and piano was premiered in Washington at the invitation of the Smithsonian Institution.

As a performer, Capers has appeared with outstanding artists such as Dizzy Gillespie, Ray Brown, Wynton Marsalis, Mongo Santamaria, Max Roach, and Paquito D'Rivera. On National Public Radio, she has appeared on Marian McPartland's *Piano Jazz* and Branford Marsalis's *Jazzset*. With her trio, she has played at colleges, universities, and clubs throughout the country, has appeared on radio and television, and has been heard in concert at many major music halls. The trio's performances received rave reviews at the International Grande Parade de Jazz Festival in Nice, the Martin Luther King Festival in Ottawa, and the North Sea Jazz Festival in The Hague. The trio has also participated in the Monterey Festival, the Mellon Festival, New York's Kool and JVC Jazz Festivals, and the Norfolk Chamber Music Festival in New Haven. As a classical soloist, Capers has played Mozart's Piano Concerto No. 23 at the Malibu Music Festival.

Widely known and respected as an innovative educator, Capers has conducted jazz workshops and lecture-concerts nationwide, in addition to her college and conservatory teaching. Capers can be heard—as composer, arranger, pianist, and singer—on four recordings: *Portrait in Soul* (Atlantic), *Affirmation* (KMA Arts), *Come On Home* (Columbia Artists), and *Wagner Takes the A Train* (Elysium). At home in New York City, she is often heard at her favorite club, the Knickerbocker.